THIS BOOK BELONGS TO:

FORT WORTH LIBRARY

W9-AAE-252

For Mom and Dad, who taught me how to draw.
And how to do everything else too.
– Jarom

Horses: Wild & Tame © Flying Eye Books 2017.

This is a first edition published in 2017 by Flying Eye Books,
an imprint of Nobrow Ltd. 27 Westgate Street, London E8 3RL.

Illustrations © Jarom Vogel 2017.
Jarom Vogel has asserted his right under the Copyright, Designs
and Patents Act, 1988, to be identified as the Illustrator of this Work.

Iris Volant is the pen name of the Flying Eye Books in-house writers.
Text written by Hanna Milner.

All rights reserved. No part of this publication may be reproduced
or transmitted in any form or by any means, electronic or mechanical,
including photocopying, recording or by any information and storage
retrieval system, without prior written consent from the publisher.

Published in the US by Nobrow (US) Inc.
Printed in Latvia on FSC® certified paper.

FSC
www.fsc.org

MIX
Paper from
responsible sources
FSC® C002795

ISBN: 978-1-911171-89-8
Order from www.flyingeyebooks.com

IRIS VOLANT   JAROM VOGEL

HORSES
WILD & TAME

FLYING EYE BOOKS
LONDON | NEW YORK

CONTENTS

INTRODUCTION

The proud and beautiful horse has been a part of humans' lives for many thousands of years. We have admired them from our earliest cave paintings to modern movies and books. In fact, the story of human progress is linked in many ways to the horse – we have used them to farm our land, fight in wars, carry heavy goods, and take us to new places.

Although the horse has mostly been used as a working animal, it is clear that there is more to our relationship with these elegant creatures. Many people who work with horses or care for them will tell you about the strong bond they form with their animals.

In this book, we'll see how the modern horse evolved, discover the many ways that horses and humans have worked together, and meet some of the most famous horses from history.

The dawn horse

WHAT IS A HORSE?

Horses evolved over millions of years from a small, dog-sized mammal that lived in North America. Scientists have called it Eohippus, 'the dawn horse'. The dawn horse had four-hoofed toes on its front feet and three-hoofed toes on its back feet.

EVOLUTION OF THE HOOF

Over 60 million years, the dawn horse's hooves evolved. The extra toes shrunk away and slowly developed into one large hoof.

The hoof is made up of two separate parts: the hard, flexible outer layer and the soft interior of skin and bone.

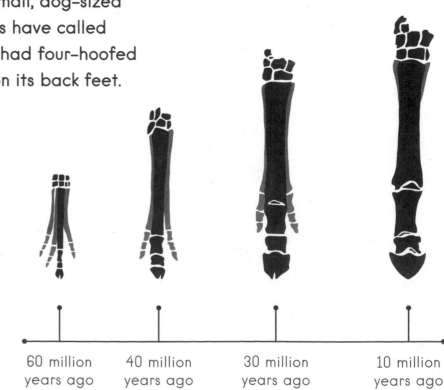

| 60 million years ago | 40 million years ago | 30 million years ago | 10 million years ago |

HORSE CHARACTER

Even though horses are mammals and by definition
'hot blooded', (instead of 'cold blooded' like reptiles),
we use the terms 'hot bloods', 'cold bloods', and
'warmbloods' to describe their different characters.

1. Clydesdale

2. Akhal-Teke

3. Norwegian Fjord

1. Cold bloods are calm and
patient. Their great strength
and size mean that they make
excellent work horses.

2. Hot bloods are bred for
speed. They have longer legs
and a bold, spirited character.

3. Warmbloods are strong and
agile, making them the perfect
horses for riding.

HORSE GAITS

Horses can move in four ways, called 'gaits'.
Here you can see the different strides a horse takes in each gait.

1. Walk – The slowest gait, which is used for strolling around the field.

2. Trot – Used by working horses, as it does not use up too much energy.

3. Canter – A faster, controlled gait that sounds like three quick beats.

4. Gallop – The fastest speed. Can only be used for short distances before they need to rest.

WILD HORSES

Thousands of years ago, all horses were wild animals. They roamed free across parts of Asia and Europe, along the vast grasslands and savannas of the Eurasian Steppe.

Today, almost all horses are domesticated, which means that they have been tamed by humans and used for work or sport. Many archeologists trace the first domesticated horses to Central Asia, around 6,000 years ago.

THE TAKHI

Modern horses are all descended from wild horses like the Mongolian wild horse, known as the takhi. There are also many populations of feral horses around the world, but these are descended from domesticated groups that now roam freely. The takhi was extinct in the wild until quite recently. It has now returned to its home in Mongolia due to conservation work across the world.

PREHISTORIC PAINTINGS

The first pictures of the horse are cave paintings from about 30,000 years ago. These horses were wild animals and were probably hunted for their meat, alongside bison and mammoths. The paintings in Chauvet cave, France, are the oldest in the world. The famous 'horse panel' was made by scraping charcoal across the surface of the rock.

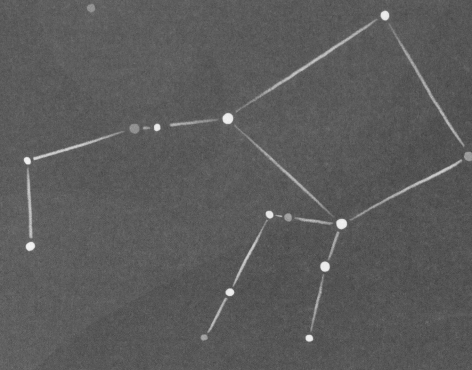

LEGENDARY HORSE: PEGASUS

From ancient myths to modern stories, humankind's close relationship with horses can be seen throughout history. Often representing faithfulness, power and freedom, horses have become immortalized in tales that are still told today.

One of the most famous animals from the Greek myths was a winged horse called Pegasus. According to the legends, Pegasus had divine powers and was tasked with carrying Zeus' thunderbolts.

For his service to the king of the gods, Zeus transformed him into stars. The Pegasus constellation is visible in the northern sky.

WAR HORSES

Around 4000 BC, horses began to be used in warfare. From Ancient Egyptian chariots to the mounted cavalry of World War I, horses have carried humans into countless battles.

Ancient Egyptian chariot racing into battle

THE SADDLE

The invention of the saddle played a hugely important role, as it allowed people to ride horses into battle more securely and comfortably. The Romans were the first to create proper saddles, made of solid wood and bound in leather. The saddles spread the weight of the rider across the horse's back so that it could be ridden for longer, and the shape of the saddle meant that riders were less likely to fall off.

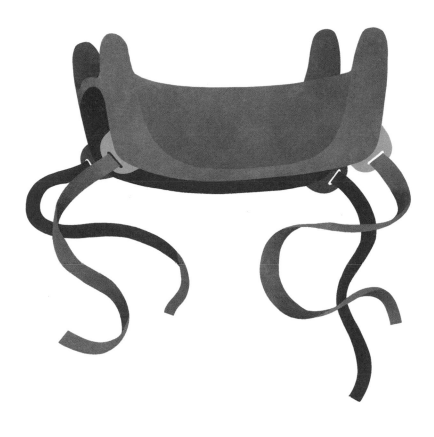

Saddle based on Roman design

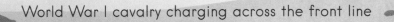

World War I cavalry charging across the front line

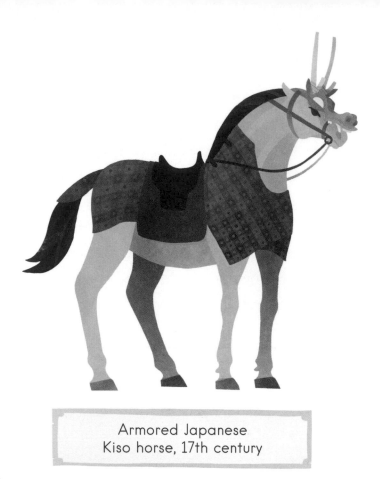

Armored Japanese
Kiso horse, 17th century

Austrian armor for the Holy Roman Emperor's
horse, probably a Kladruber, 16th century

MEDIEVAL CAVALRY

The careful breeding of different types of war horses – heavy and large in Europe; lean and fast in Asia – has led to many varied breeds across the world.

The knights that fought in the medieval Crusades from the 11th to 16th century rode expensive warhorses called destriers.

These were not a specific breed, but rather a type of horse – powerful, courageous, and trained for war from an early age. Destriers had to be fast and agile, but also big and strong enough to support a heavily armored knight on the battlefield.

Armored Mongol horse,
13th century

Arabian horse in Ottoman
armor, 16th century

European destrier in full armor
with knight, 14th century

ROYAL STEEDS

Native to west India, the rare Marwari horse was the warhorse of choice for the royal Rajput clans. During the Battle of Haldighati in 1576, the opposing Mughal soldiers rode upon great elephants, so the Rajputs made fake trunks for their horses to wear. This confused the elephants, as they wouldn't attack what looked to them like baby elephants! The Rajput ruler's horse, Chetak, is famous for carrying his master away to safety even though he was badly injured. Marwari horses are now legendary for their bravery in battle and loyalty to their riders.

FAMOUS HORSE: BUCEPHALUS

Alexander the Great of Macedonia ruled one of the biggest empires in the ancient world, and the horse he rode into every battle may be the most famous in ancient history. Bucephalus was a huge and powerful Thessalian horse, with a black coat and unusual blue eyes. According to ancient writers, Alexander was the only man able to tame him.

Alexander understood horse behavior and knew that they often fear shadows. By gently touching Bucephalus and turning him away from his own shadow, Alexander was able to calm the horse's nerves. Today, we would call this 'horse whispering', which is a natural method of training horses.

WORK HORSES

In the age before machinery, horses were a crucial part of working life. They worked on farmers' fields and carried the goods of traveling merchants for hundreds of miles.

TRAVEL AND TRANSPORT

As time passed, horses were used in new ways. 'Flying coaches' carried people through the streets of Europe and America. Just before cars took over, horses were even used to pull double-decker buses!

Around 1740, a vast network of canals was built across Britain. Canal horses were used to pull boats laden with goods. This was the main way of transporting goods across the country until the construction of the railroad system.

LOGGING

Work horses are used today for certain tasks that cannot be performed by machinery, for example logging in densely forested areas that are beyond the reach of tractors. Using machinery would cause damage to the woodland, but horse loggers are more environmentally friendly.

BUFFALO HORSES

When European settlers arrived in North America on horseback in 1519, the Native American peoples had never seen such strange animals before. However, by the late 1600s they had begun to adopt horses into their own culture and soon became very skillful riders.

Horses changed Native American communities in many ways. The tribes could now travel greater distances, and most importantly, horses helped with buffalo hunting. In fact, the Nez Perce people bred special 'buffalo horses' just for this purpose, like the beautiful spotted Appaloosa.

LEGENDARY HORSE: BLACK BEAUTY

When Anna Sewell wrote the novel Black Beauty in 1877, it completely changed people's attitudes towards working horses. The fashion at the time in Victorian England was for horses to look proud and spirited, so cab drivers used a piece of equipment called a 'bearing rein' to keep the horse's head very high. This device was strapped around the horse's neck and head, forcing the horse into an unnatural position and causing pain.

Black Beauty is written from the perspective of a hard-working horse and brings attention to the mistreatment of work horses. The book encouraged people to be kinder towards horses, leading to many new laws in England and America that now protect these beautiful animals.

SPORTS HORSES

Humans have probably raced horses ever since the earliest days of domestication. The first formal races appeared in Ancient Greece, where people raced horse–drawn chariots in specially built stadiums called hippodromes.

ANCIENT CHARIOT RACES

In 680 BC, chariot racing became an official sport in the ancient Olympic Games. The Romans loved chariot racing so much that they built the Circus Maximus, a huge stadium with over 150,000 seats, as a venue to watch the sport.

A Spartan princess called Cynisca was the first woman ever to be awarded the wreath of victory in 396 BC. Although women were not allowed to officially compete in the ancient Olympic Games, Cynisca owned and trained her team of winning horses.

MODERN OLYMPICS

Horses are still seen in the Olympics today but instead of pulling chariots in a race, horses and their riders are judged on their ability to work together with speed and grace.

Dressage is a very formal type of riding, where the horse and rider perform various movements in a skilled and seemingly effortless way.

A horse and rider demonstrating a 'canter pirouette'

In show jumping, horses and their riders must leap over gates and fences that are easily knocked down. They lose points every time an obstacle is knocked over.

NAADAM FESTIVAL

In Mongolia, there are more horses than there are people. The biggest event of the year is the Naadam festival, where children as young as five compete in horse races. The losing horse is called 'full stomach'.

Race horses are bred specifically for sporting competitions. These horses are strong, fast and warmblooded. They are also usually indoor horses and form very close relationships with their riders.

FAMOUS HORSE: SEABISCUIT

Seabiscuit was a racehorse who became a great champion. He was quite small for a racehorse and was considered too lazy, but his new trainer knew that he just needed to be treated better. Very soon, Seabiscuit began to rise to success.

A defining moment in Seabiscuit's career took place in 1938, when he raced one-on-one against War Admiral, the fastest racehorse around. No one could believe it when Seabiscuit sprinted to the finish line at the last moment, overtaking the previous champion. This plucky horse became a symbol of hope, no matter what the odds.

HORSE CARE

Today, horses are mainly used for sport or leisure. A horse needs a lot of outside space and most owners need to rent a stable as well.

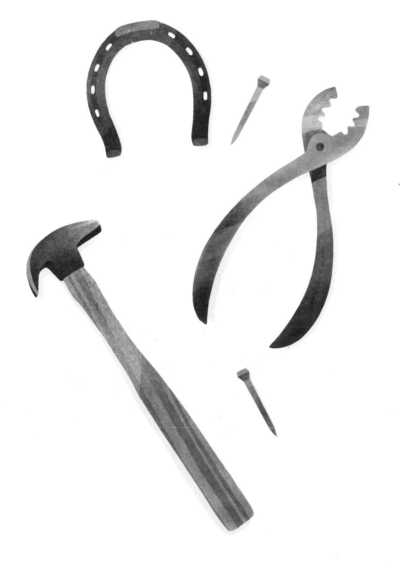

HORSESHOES

In the wild, horses live in dry climates and travel for many miles a day, making their hooves naturally hard and smooth. Domesticated horses often live in wetter climates and don't roam around as much, which means that their hooves can become soft. Specially trained people called farriers hammer metal guards onto horses' hooves to protect them and make them stronger. This doesn't hurt the horse – it's like a heavy-duty pedicure!

INDEX OF HORSES

Takhi p14-15

Thessalian p26

Mongol p22

Kiso p22

Arabian p22

Eohippus,
'the dawn horse' p10

Akhal-Teke p11

Clydesdale p11

Appaloosa
p30

Destrier p23

Pegasus p18

Kladruber p22

Norwegian
Fjord p11

Marwari p24

Thoroughbred p32, 40

45

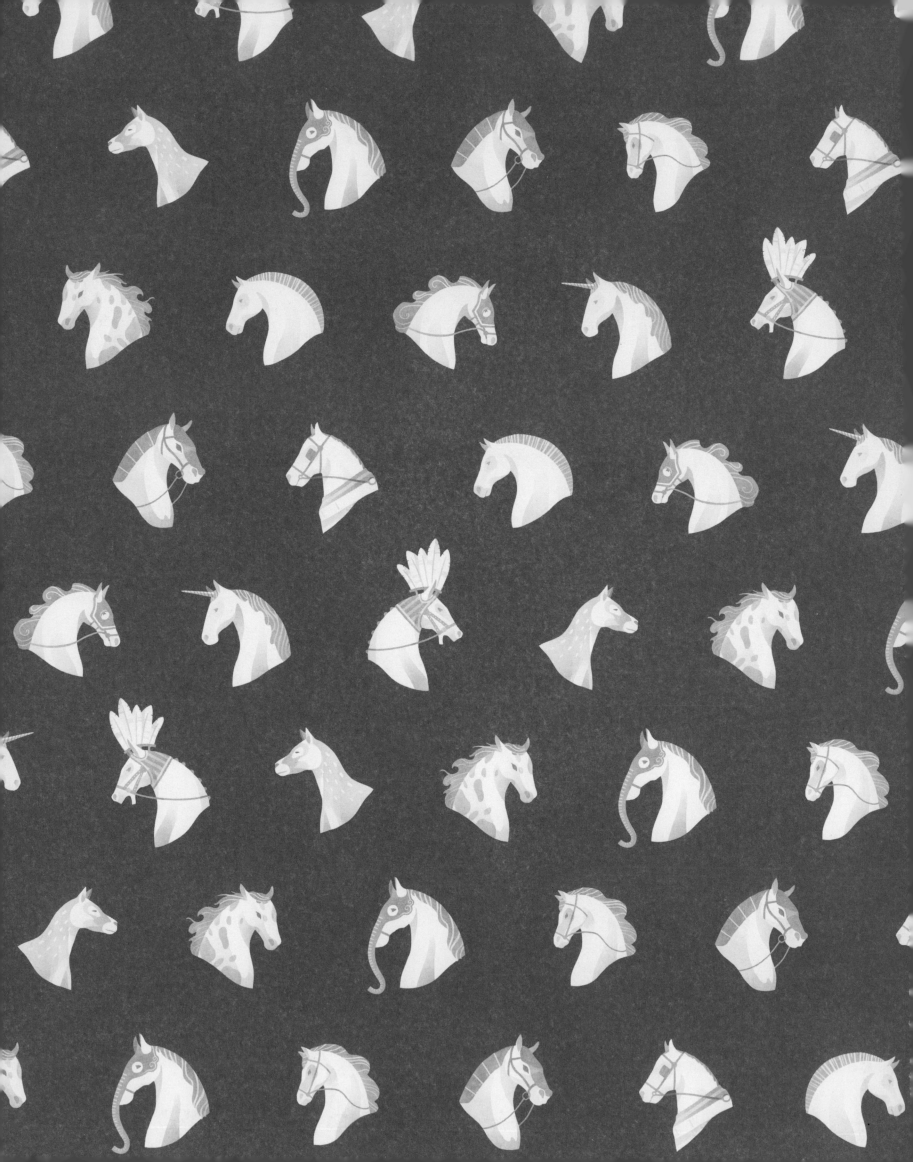